1400083

612.2
Sti   Stille, Darlene R.

          The respiratory
          system

DUE DATE	BRODART	04/01	22.00

THE RESPIRATORY SYSTEM

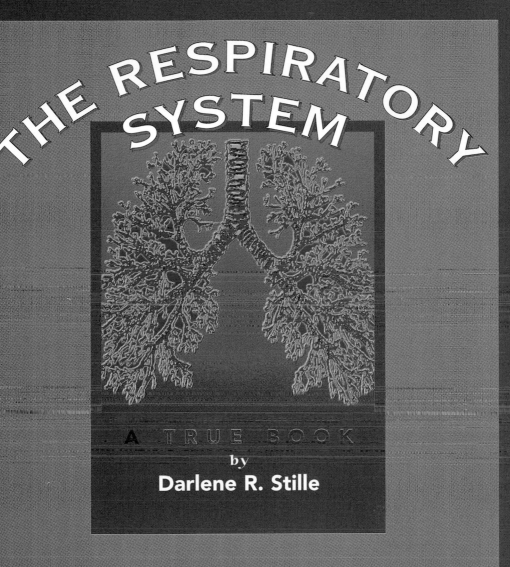

A TRUE BOOK

by
Darlene R. Stille

Children's Press®
A Division of Grolier Publishing
New York London Hong Kong Sydney
Danbury, Connecticut

Reading Consultant
Linda Cornwell
Learning Resource Consultant
Indiana Department of Education

Science Consultant
Ronald W. Schwizer, Ph.D.
Science Chair
Poly Prep Country Day School
Brooklyn, New York

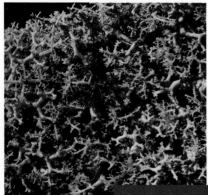

A section of lung tissue showing arteries (red), veins (blue), and alveoli (white)

Library of Congress Cataloging-in-Publication Data

Stille, Darlene R.
   The respiratory system / by Darlene R. Stille.
      p.   cm. — (True book)
   Includes bibliographical references and index.
   Summary: Describes the various parts of the human respiratory system and then explains how that system brings fresh oxygen into the body and carries carbon dioxide to the lungs to be expelled.
   ISBN 0-516-20448-3 (lib. bdg.)   0-516-26276-9 (pbk.)
   1. Respiratory organs—Juvenile literature. 2. Respiration—Juvenile literature. [1. Respiratory system. 2. Respiration.] I. Title. II. Series.
QP121.S83 1997
612.2—dc21   96-29746
                                                                              CIP
                                                                              AC

Contents

Take a Breath

What is more important—breathing in or breathing out? That's a trick question. The answer is that they are both equally important.

Take a deep breath. Feel what happens. The air enters your body through your nose or mouth. Then it goes down a tube in your neck called the windpipe, and into your lungs.

Your chest fills out as you take in air. This is because the air is filling up your lungs, which are in your chest. When your lungs are full, you cannot take in any more air.

You can hold your breath for a little while. But soon, you must breathe out. Feel what happens as your breath

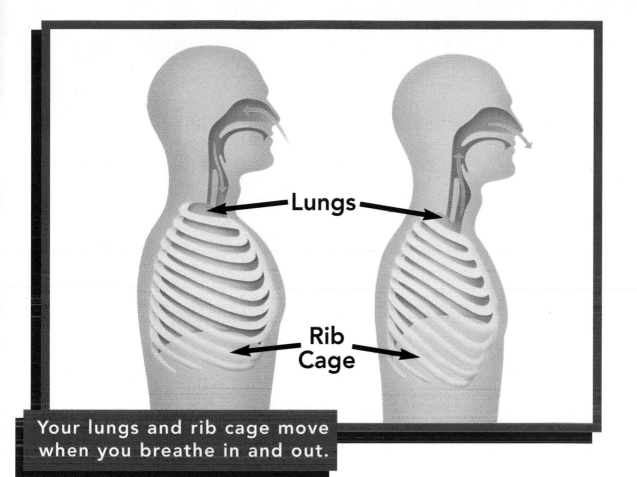

Lungs

Rib
Cage

Your lungs and rib cage move
when you breathe in and out.

leaves your lungs and goes out
through your nose or mouth.
Usually, we breathe without
even thinking about it. We

Breathing happens automatically, even when we are asleep.

breathe all the time. We breathe when we are awake and when we are asleep. We never have to think about breathing. It is so important to life that it happens automatically.

What Is Air?

We use the word *air* all the time, but what is it?

Air is a mixture of gases that are all around us. For human life, the most important of these gases is called oxygen. When we breathe in, or inhale, we are taking oxygen into our bodies.

We can't see air, but there are ways to tell that it is all around us.

Another important gas in the air around us is carbon dioxide. When we breathe out, or exhale, we breathe out carbon dioxide. All animals take in oxygen and give off carbon dioxide.

Carbon dioxide is the most important gas for plant life. Plants take in carbon dioxide and give off oxygen. This wonderful cycle is one of the things that make life on Earth possible.

Plants take in carbon dioxide and give off oxygen.

The process of taking in oxygen and giving off carbon dioxide is called respiration. In animals, the system that is responsible for breathing in and breathing out is called the respiratory system.

Our bodies must take oxygen from the air we breathe. This is because the cells in our bodies use oxygen and food to make energy. This energy keeps us alive.

Journey to the Lungs

If we could be inhaled with a breath of air and begin the journey to the lungs, we would take a very interesting ride. We might enter through the nose, trying not to be caught by tiny waving hairs whose job it is to trap dust and bacteria.

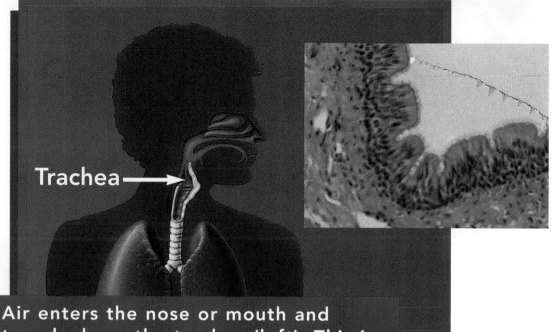

Trachea ──→

Air enters the nose or mouth and travels down the trachea (left). This is a magnified view of tiny hairs that line the inside of the nose (right).

We would then tumble past the voice box and into a long, dark tube called the windpipe, or trachea. At the end of the windpipe, there are two branching tunnels. One goes to the left, and the other goes to the right. But it doesn't matter which tunnel we take, because each tunnel leads to one of our two lungs.

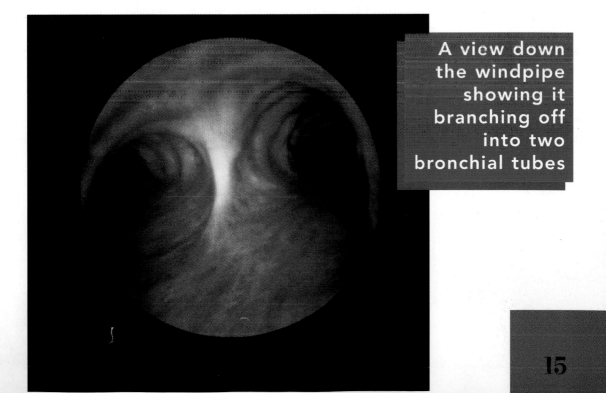

A view down the windpipe showing it branching off into two bronchial tubes

These tunnels are called bronchial tubes. As we go, we see the tunnel divide again and again. Each new tunnel is smaller than the last one.

If we could step outside and look at the tunnels, we would see what looks like an upside-down tree. In fact, the whole thing is called the bronchial tree! The "trunk" is the trachea, and the main "branches" are the bronchial tubes. The small-er "branches" and "twigs" are

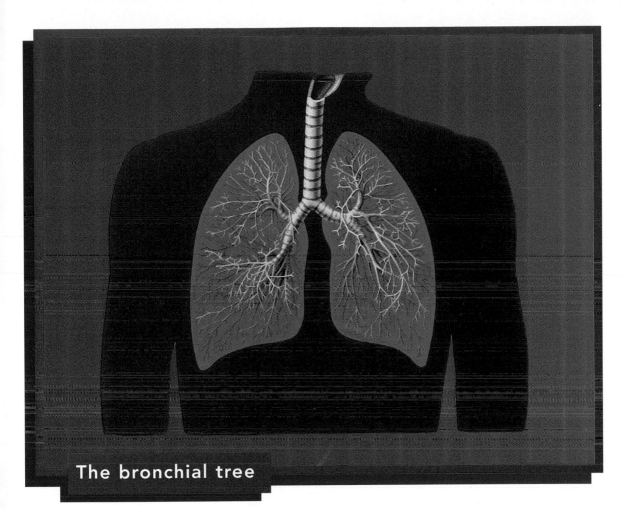

The bronchial tree

called bronchioles. The
smallest twigs of the bronchial
tree end inside the lungs.

17

Inside the Lungs

At last, we squeeze out of a tiny tunnel at the end of the bronchial tree and enter the lung itself. What a strange place this is. It is like being inside a big sponge!

But when we look closely, we see that the spongy lung tissue is made up of many

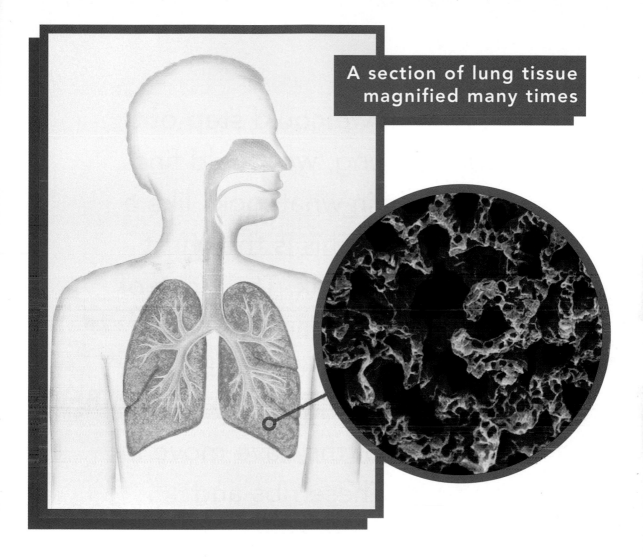

A section of lung tissue magnified many times

tiny sacs filled with air. The walls of these air sacs are very thin.

Now, if we could step out-side the lung, we would find ourselves in what looks like a large cave. This is the chest cavity, or thorax. The sides of the cave are made of thick bands of muscle, and bones called ribs. With every breath, the walls of the cave move in and out. These ribs and muscles in the chest wall protect the lungs from injury.

At the bottom of the chest cavity opposite the bronchial

With every breath, the walls of the chest cavity move in and out (left). This diagram shows how the diaphragm moves during breathing (right).

tree is another wall of muscle called the diaphragm. The diaphragm separates the chest cavity from another large space, the abdominal cavity.

The right lung is divided into three parts. The left lung is divided into two.

The space inside the chest cavity is almost completely filled by the lungs. One lung is on the left side of the chest, and the other lung is on the right side. The right and left lungs look slightly different. The right lung has three divisions, called lobes, while the left lung has two.

But each lobe looks the same inside. It is a mass of tiny air sacs. These air sacs are called alveoli. The job of

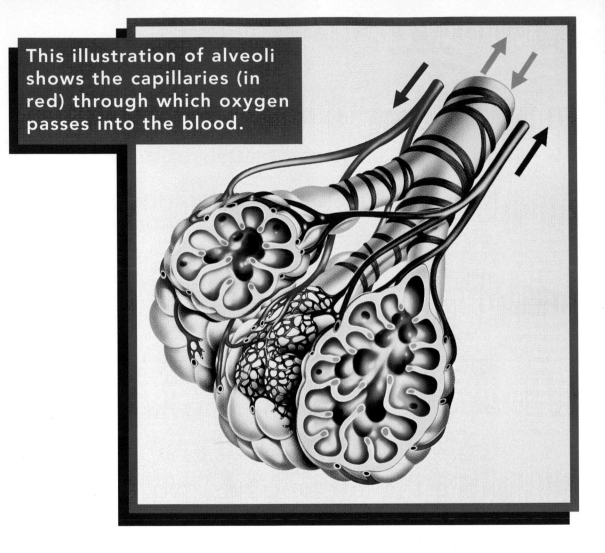

This illustration of alveoli shows the capillaries (in red) through which oxygen passes into the blood.

the alveoli is to put oxygen into the blood and take carbon dioxide out.

In the walls of the alveoli
are tiny blood vessels called
capillaries. When you breathe
in oxygen, it is stored briefly
in the alveoli. Then the
oxygen passes into a capillary
and enters a red blood cell.

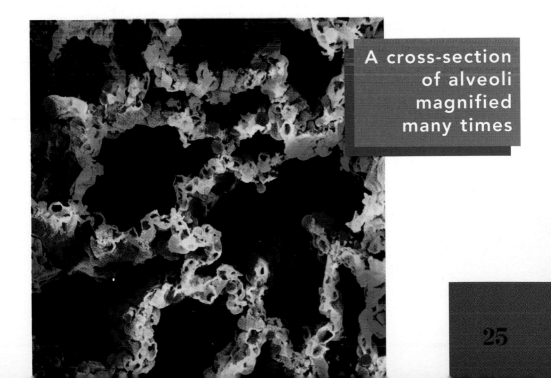

A cross-section
of alveoli
magnified
many times

Where the Heart Fits In

After the oxygen "hitches a ride" inside a red blood cell, it is carried away from the lungs by blood. This is where the heart fits in. The heart plays a big role in pumping the blood all over the body.

The oxygen-rich blood is pumped into the heart and

This photograph shows three red blood cells along an alveolar wall.

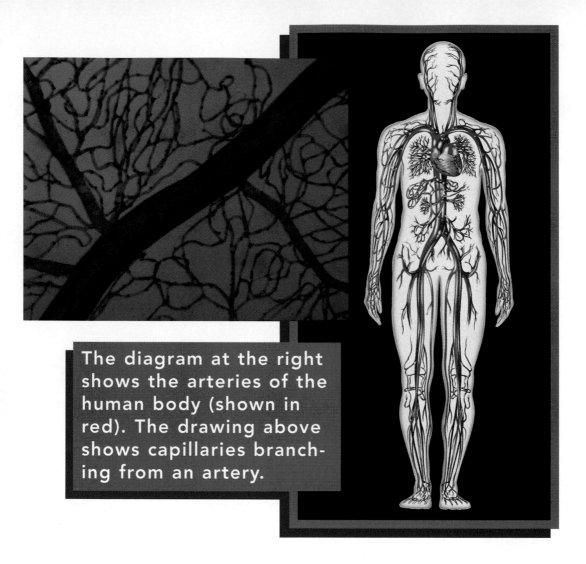

The diagram at the right shows the arteries of the human body (shown in red). The drawing above shows capillaries branching from an artery.

then out to every part of the body through blood vessels called arteries. Arteries begin in the heart and branch out into smaller and smaller blood vessels that eventually reach every cell.

When oxygen reaches the smallest type of blood vessel—a capillary—it passes through the capillary wall and into a nearby cell.

A photograph of red blood cells traveling through a capillary

Carbon Dioxide in Our Bodies

Our cells use oxygen while food is broken down to provide energy. When this happens, the cells give off waste products. A chief waste product is carbon dioxide. Our bodies must get rid of this gas.

The way the body gets rid of carbon dioxide is just the

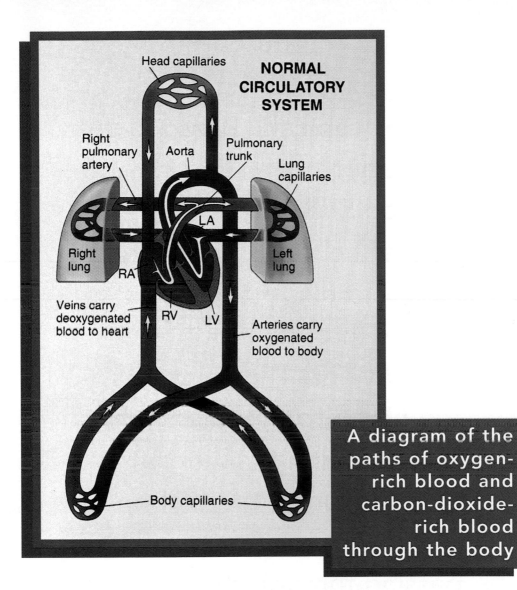

Head capillaries

NORMAL CIRCULATORY SYSTEM

Right pulmonary artery

Aorta

Pulmonary trunk

Lung capillaries

LA

Right lung

RA

Left lung

Veins carry deoxygenated blood to heart

RV

LV

Arteries carry oxygenated blood to body

Body capillaries

A diagram of the paths of oxygen-rich blood and carbon-dioxide-rich blood through the body

opposite of how it takes in oxygen. Carbon dioxide leaves a cell and enters a nearby capillary. Blood in the capillary picks up the carbon dioxide and begins the return trip to the heart. Carrying carbon dioxide, the blood travels through blood vessels called veins. The veins deliver the blood to the heart, which pumps it into the lungs.

In the lungs, the carbon dioxide leaves the blood by passing through the wall of a capillary and into the lung's tiny air sacs. When we exhale,

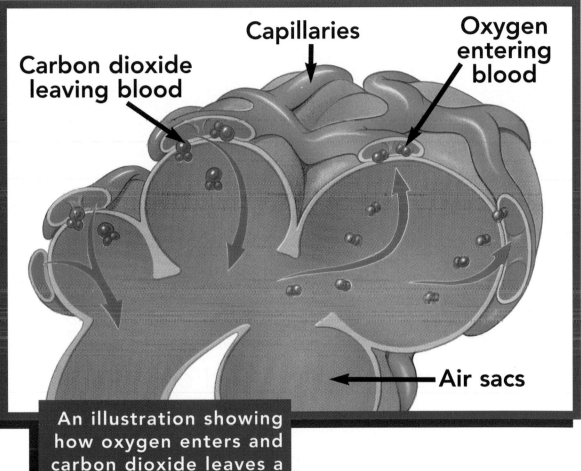

Carbon dioxide leaving blood

Capillaries

Oxygen entering blood

Air sacs

An illustration showing how oxygen enters and carbon dioxide leaves a capillary in the lung

Boys exhaling air on a cold day

we breathe out air containing the carbon dioxide. Then, as we breathe in, blood brought by the heart to the lungs picks up a fresh supply of oxygen—and the process starts all over again.

Keeping Our Lungs Healthy

We all know how it feels when germs cause infection in our respiratory system. We cough and sneeze and have a runny nose. These are symptoms of a cold or the flu. Resting and drinking plenty of liquids can help

An infection in your respiratory system may make you cough or sneeze.

with the symptoms, and people usually get better in about a week.

But some infections of the respiratory system are more serious. Germs in the bronchial tree can cause an infection called bronchitis. A person with bronchitis coughs all the time because the bronchial tubes fill with a sticky fluid called mucus. Doctors can treat this infection with antibiotics.

Asthma

People with asthma have a hard time breathing. When they breathe, they make a wheezing sound, because asthma causes the bronchial tubes to constrict. A severe asthma attack may require a trip to the emergency room.

Asthma is often caused by allergies to dust, mold, or pollen. Avoiding these things can help prevent asthma attacks.

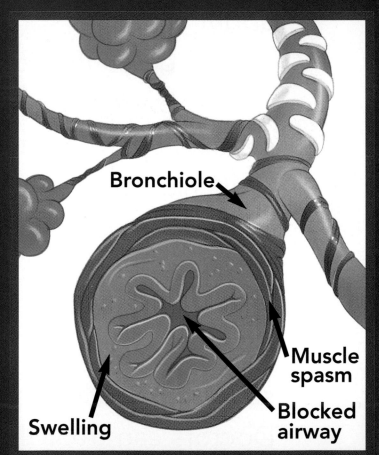

Bronchiole

Swelling

Muscle spasm

Blocked airway

Doctors can prescribe medication to help prevent asthma attacks. With good medical care, a person with asthma can lead a normal life.

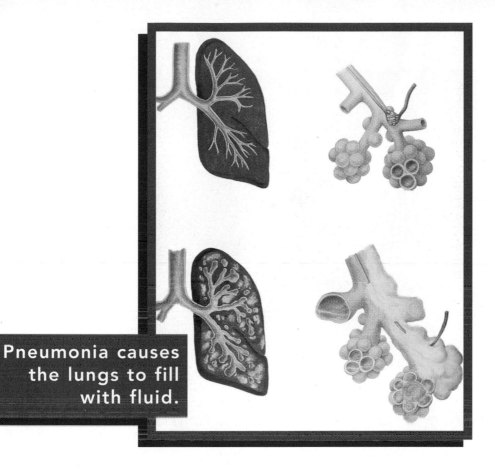

Pneumonia causes the lungs to fill with fluid.

The most serious infections of the lungs are pneumonia and tuberculosis. These diseases can also be treated with antibiotics.

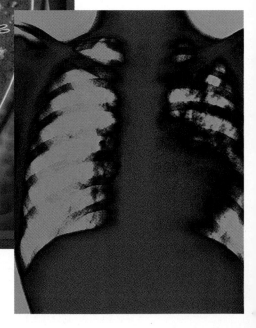

The drawing above shows how tuberculosis damages a person's lungs. At right is a false-color chest X-ray of a person with tuberculosis.

Other serious disorders of the lungs, such as cancer, are not caused by germs. They are caused mainly by breathing in polluted air, asbestos, and tobacco smoke.

It is hard to protect ourselves from colds or flu. But it is easier to protect ourselves from lung cancer and another serious lung disease called emphysema. Medical researchers say

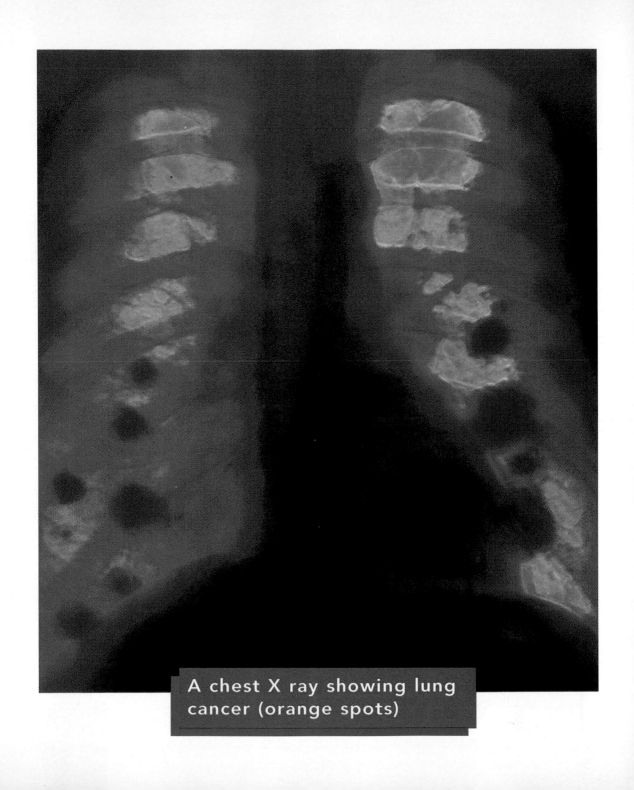

A chest X ray showing lung cancer (orange spots)

most cases of cancer and emphysema are caused by smoking cigarettes. So the solution is simple: don't smoke and you will have a good chance of breathing easily all your life.

To Find Out More

Here are some additional resources to help you learn more about the respiratory system:

Books

Adler, David A. **You Breathe In, You Breathe Out: All About Your Lungs.** Franklin Watts, 1991.

Ganeri, Anita. **Breathing**. Raintree Steck-Vaughn, 1995.

Parker, Steve. **The Lungs and Breathing.** Franklin Watts, 1989.

Richardson, Joy. **What Happens When You Breathe?** Gareth Stevens Publishing, 1986.

Markle, Sandra. **Outside and Inside You.** Bradbury Press, 1991.

Organizations

American Lung Association
1740 Broadway
New York, NY 10019-4374
800-LUNG-USA

The Exploratorium
3601 Lyon Street
San Francisco, CA 94123
415-563-7337

**The Franklin Institute
Science Museum**
222 North 20th Street
Philadelphia, PA 19103
215-448-1200

**Museum of Health and
Medical Science**
1515 Hermann Drive
Houston, TX 77004
713-521-1515

**Museum of Science
and Industry**
57th Street & Lake Shore Dr.
Chicago, IL
773-684-1414

**National Heart, Lung, and
Blood Institute**
P.O. Box 30105
Bethesda, MD 20824-0105
301-251-1223 (fax)

Internet Sites

ExploraNet
*http://www. exploratorium.
edu/*

Visit a constantly changing
assortment of online
exhibits presented by the
Exploratorium

**The Museum of Health
and Medical Science**
*http://www. mhms.org/
enter.html*

Visit the "Amazing Body
Pavilion" to explore the
heart, lungs, digestive
system, and more.

Important Words

antibiotics drugs that control diseases by killing the bacteria that cause them

asbestos mineral once commonly used to make fireproof materials

bacteria tiny, one-celled organisms; some kinds cause infections

constrict to tighten

cross section a slice or piece cut straight across something

diaphragm muscular wall separating the chest from the abdomen

emphysema disease in which the many tiny sacs inside the lungs become fewer and larger, which causes breathing to become more and more difficult

pneumonia a disease, caused by infection, in which one or both lungs become swollen and irritated

sac bag

Index

Meet the Author

Darlene Stille lives in Chicago and is executive editor of the *World Book Annuals* and World Book's Online Service. She has written several Children's Press books, including *Extraordinary Women Scientists, Extraordinary Women of Medicine,* and three other True Books on the body systems.